12 POETS WHO CHANGED THE WORLD

by Allan Morey

12 STORY LIBRARY
MORE TO EXPLORE

www.12StoryLibrary.com

12-Story Library is an imprint of Bookstaves.

Photographs ©: G. Frank E. Pearsall/PD, cover, 1; PD, 4; The George W. Elkins Collection, 1924/PD, 4; PD, 5-7; Chyah/PD, 8; Yury Zap/Shutterstock.com, 8; Daderot/PD, 9; PD, 10; Daderot/PD, 11; JoJan/CC3.0, 11; National Library of Wales/PD, 12; PD, 12; Mike Peel/CC4.0, 13; G. Frank E. Pearsall/PD, 14; PD, 15; Thayer and Eldridge/PD, 15; PD, 16; National Library of Scotland/PD, 17; Christie's/PD, 17; PD, 18-21; Science History Images/Alamy, 22; CBW/Alamy, 23; PD, 23; Everett Collection Inc/Alamy, 24; Tribune Content Agency LLC/Alamy, 25; PD, 25; Eric Koch/Anefo/PD, 26; Carolmooredc/CC4.0, 27; Georgios Kollidas/Shutterstock.com, 28; SLOWKING/CC3.0, 29

ISBN
9781632357199 (hardcover)
9781632358288 (paperback)
9781645820079 (ebook)

Library of Congress Control Number: 2019938645

Printed in the United States of America
July 2019

About the Cover
Walt Whitman circa 1869.

Access free, up-to-date content on this topic plus a full digital version of this book. Scan the QR code on page 31 or use your school's login at 12StoryLibrary.com.

Table of Contents

1

Homer: Father of Western Literature

Thousands of years ago, people did not read for entertainment. They listened to storytellers. Storytellers traveled from village to village. They told tales of mythical heroes and great battles. These myths were part of an oral tradition. They were passed from one generation to the next by word of mouth. The Greek poet Homer was one of the first to write down these ancient stories.

Not a lot is known of Homer. He lived nearly 3,000 years ago. He is believed to have written the *Iliad* and the *Odyssey*. These two books are epic poems. They are written in verse and they tell stories.

A Reading from Homer, painted by Lawrence Alma-Tadema.

1200 BCE

Approximate year when the real Trojan War was fought

- The city of Troy was in modern-day Turkey.
- Many words and phrases we use today come from ancient myths. A Trojan Horse is something meant to secretly defeat an enemy.
- The epic poem *Iliad* is 10,000 lines long. *Odyssey* is 15,000 lines.

The *Iliad* tells of the Trojan War. In myths, this war was caused by a man named Paris. He was a prince from the city of Troy. He stole Queen Helen away from her husband, the Greek king Menelaus. The king then gathered an army and attacked Troy. The war went on for 10 years. It ended only after the Greek hero Odysseus snuck into Troy. He was hidden in a large statue of a wooden horse.

The *Odyssey* tells of Odysseus's journey home after the war. On his way, he battled monsters and traveled to the underworld. It took him 10 years to reach home.

It is not known when Homer died. But his books have inspired everything from comic book superheroes to stories about fantastic monsters.

The Procession of the Trojan Horse in Troy, circa 1760.

2

Li Po: China's Wandering Poet

Li Po, or Li Bo, was an ancient Chinese poet. He was born in the eighth century CE, in the year 701. Throughout his life, Po wandered around Asia. He wrote about the things he saw and the people he met.

Much of his early work was about nature. Po also liked to write about friendships, the moon, and drinking wine. People enjoyed his poems for their clear images and simple language.

When war broke out in the 750s, the subject of Po's poems changed. He sometimes wrote about his thoughts on war. In his poem "The Long War," he commented on a war that went on and on. The soldiers were very far from home. Their armor was worn out. Their horses were hungry. But the fighting continued.

Po died in 762. He is considered one of China's greatest poets.

About 1,100

Number of Li Po's poems still in existence

- It is believed that he wrote as many as 100,000 poems.
- Po often wrote a type of poem called a *yuefu.* The form is similar to ancient Chinese folk songs.
- Legends say Po drowned in a river while embracing the moon's reflection.

TANG DYNASTY

The Tang Dynasty lasted from 618 to 907. It was a golden age for Chinese culture. Music and literature were highly popular. But the period is best known for its poetry. Poets like Li Po, Tu Fu, and Wang Wei lived during the Tang Dynasty. Tu Fu wrote poems about the hardships caused by war. Wang Wei often wrote about the beauty of nature.

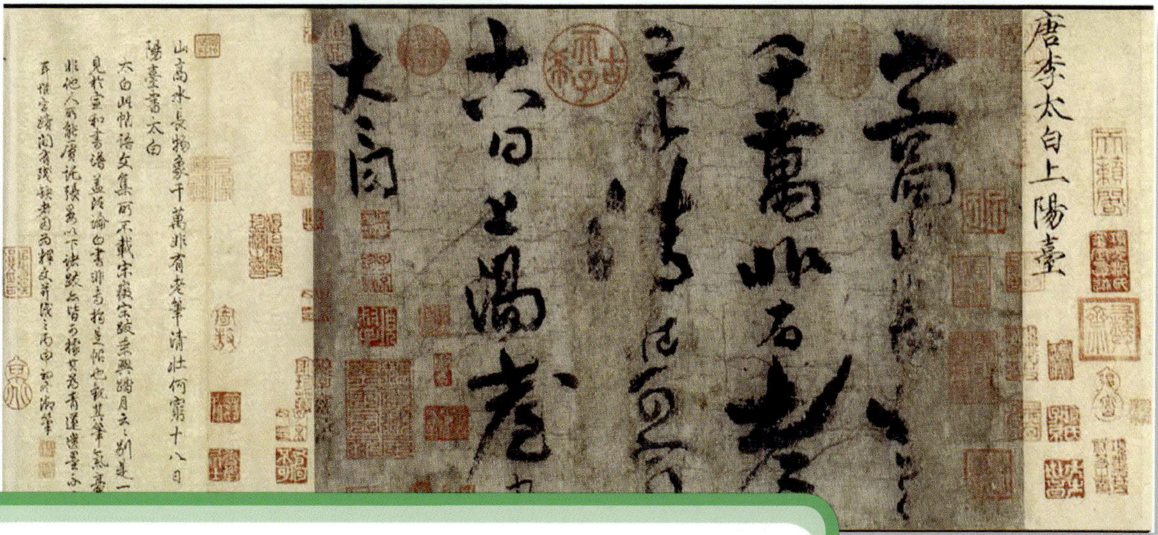

The only surviving example of Li Po's hand-written caligraphy, a poem titled "To Yangtai Temple."

3

Rumi: Inspirational Poet

From memes to posters, Rumi is one of the most quoted poets. People find his short verses about love inspiring.

Jalāl al-Dīn Rūmī was born in 1207 in what is now Afghanistan. When he was still a child, he and his family moved to present-day Turkey.

Rumi studied to be a Sufi mystic. He belonged to a very spiritual group of the Muslim religion. They believed enlightenment came through meditation and living a simple life. Love, especially love of God, was important to Sufis.

Rumi wrote his thoughts and ideas down as poems. *Masnavi* is a six-book collection of his work. Many of the poems are religious in nature. But they also speak of love and friendship. They provide simple insights on how to lead a happy life.

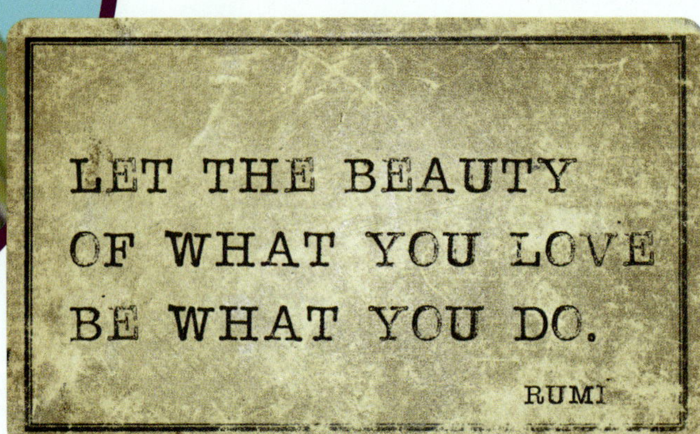

This book of Rumi's spiritual couplets is from 1603.

Rumi died in 1273. His thought-provoking words have made him one of the world's most loved poets.

GHAZAL

The ghazal is a poetry form that began in the Middle East. Ghazals are 5–15 couplets long. Each couplet has a separate idea or thought. But they are connected by a similar theme, such as love or longing. Both lines in the first couplet end in the same word or phrase. It is also the last word or phrase in all the other couplets.

2

Number of lines in a couplet

- Most of Rumi's poetry was written in couplets. The word *masnavi* means couplet in Arabic.
- Rumi did not actually write his poems. He said them aloud while someone else wrote them down.
- In 1244, Rumi met the mystic Shams Al-Dīn Tabrīzī. He wrote thousands of lines of poetry about their friendship.

4

Dante: Master Storyteller

Dante Alighieri was born in 1265 in Florence, Italy. He lived during the early years of the Renaissance. This period in European history was known for its great advancements in the arts and sciences. Dante studied painting and music. But he is best remembered for his writing.

Early in life, Dante fell in love with Beatrice Portinari. She died young. But she would inspire Dante's most famous work. *La divina commedia*, or *The Divine Comedy*, was an epic poem. It is a long poem that tells the story of a hero.

In *The Divine Comedy,* the hero is a man named Pilgrim. He is a religious traveler. He wanders through the afterlife. He sees what happens to people who do wrong. He meets spirits of the dead, from ancient poets to Beatrice. After Beatrice guides Pilgrim through Heaven, he returns to earth. He then writes a poem about his journey.

At the time, most books were written in the ancient language of Latin. Few people could read it. Dante wrote in Italian. This was a more common language. More people were able to enjoy his work.

Portrait of Dante circa 1495.

This statue of Beatrice consoling Dante is on Lake Como in Italy.

COMINCIA LACOMEDIA DI
dante alleghieri di fiorenze nellaq̃le tracta
delle pene et punitioni de uitii et demeriti
et premii delle uirtu: Capitolo primo della
pma parte de questo libro loquale sechiama
inferno: nel quale lautore fa prohemio ad
tucto eltractato del libro:.

NEL mezo delcamin dinrã uita
mi trouai puna selua oscura
che la diricta uia era smarrita
Et quanto adir q̃lera cosa dura
esta selua seluagia aspra et forte
che nel pensier renoua la paura
Tante amara che pocho piu morte
ma per tractar del ben chio uitrouai
diro dellatre cose chi uo scorte
I non so ben ridir come uentrai
tantera pien disonno insuquil punto
che la uerace uia abandonai
Ma poi che fui appie dum colle gionto
ladoue terminaua quella ualle
che mauea dipaura el cor compuncto
Guardai inalto et uidde le sue spalle
uestite gia deraggi del pianeta
che mena dricto altrui perogni calle
Allor fu la paura un pocho cheta
che nellaco del cor mera durata
la nocte chio passi contanta pieta

An original copy of *The Divine Comedy* that was printed in 1472.

Dante died in 1321. His poem *The Divine Comedy* is considered one of the greatest works of literature.

THINK ABOUT IT

Dante wrote in Italian when most books were written in ancient Latin. Why was this important? How might this have changed literature?

14,233

Number of lines in *The Divine Comedy*

- Pilgrim is really Dante. In some ways, the story tells of the poet seeing his lost love, Beatrice, in the afterlife.
- *The Divine Comedy* is divided into three parts. They are Inferno, Purgatorio, and Paradiso.
- Dante wrote *La Vita Nuova*, or *The New Life*, about his love of Beatrice.

5 William Wordsworth: Poet of the Romantic Era

Portrait of William Wordsworth from 1836.

William Wordsworth was born in 1770 in England. During his youth, he spent a lot of time playing in the outdoors. His love of nature inspired poems like "I Wandered Lonely as a Cloud."

It starts like this:

I wandered lonely as a cloud
That floats on high o'er vales and hills,
When all at once I saw a crowd,
A host of golden daffodils;
Beside the lake, beneath the trees,
Fluttering and dancing in the breeze.

Wordsworth wrote his best-known works after meeting fellow English poet Samuel Taylor Coleridge. Together, they published *Lyrical Ballads*. Wordsworth wrote most of the poems. But the most important part of the book was the preface. There, Wordsworth mentioned his thoughts on poetry. He felt poems could express ideas and feelings about

Samuel Taylor Coleridge.

ROMANTICISM

Romanticism was an artistic movement that began in the late 1700s. Before then, poets based much of their work on ancient Greek and Roman literature. But Romantic poets wrote about everyday life. They wrote about nature and politics. They also wrote poems of love and passion. For them, poetry was a way to express feelings.

the world. He thought poems should be about everyday life and common people. He also wanted to write poetry using conversational language. He believed it should sound similar to how people talked. These were all new ideas for the time.

Wordsworth died in 1850. His ideas helped bring about the Romantic era in poetry.

1798

Year when Wordsworth met Coleridge

- Wordsworth was the British poet laureate from 1843 to 1850.
- 1798 began a period for Wordsworth known as the "great decade." Over the next 10 years, he wrote some of his most influential work.
- "The Rime of the Ancient Mariner" is one of Coleridge's best-known poems.

Wordsworth's writing desk at Dove Cottage, where he lived from 1799–1808.

6

Walt Whitman: America's Poet

Walt Whitman circa 1869.

Early on, the United States did not have art it could really call its own. Much of the country's culture was borrowed from Europe. But poet Walt Whitman would change that. He wrote poetry that was uniquely American.

Whitman was born in 1819 on Long Island, New York. He quit school at age 11 and went to work as an office boy. At 12, he learned the printing trade. He worked on-and-off in the printing industry for much of his life. His job helped fuel a love of words. He read a lot. Whitman also worked as a teacher and a journalist. He jotted down poems. In 1855, he published the first version of *Leaves of Grass*.

Few people at the time appreciated Whitman's work. His poems were unlike most poetry of the day. He did not use meter or rhyme. This style of poetry would be called free verse.

Throughout his life, Whitman worked on *Leaves of Grass*. He continued to add more poems. His poetry was often about things he saw. He traveled a lot. So he wrote about the American countryside. His poems also told of the hard-working people and soldiers he met. Unlike most poets before him, Whitman did not romanticize war. He gave an honest view of the hardships and suffering soldiers faced.

Whitman died in 1892. His free verse was a distinctly American style of poetry.

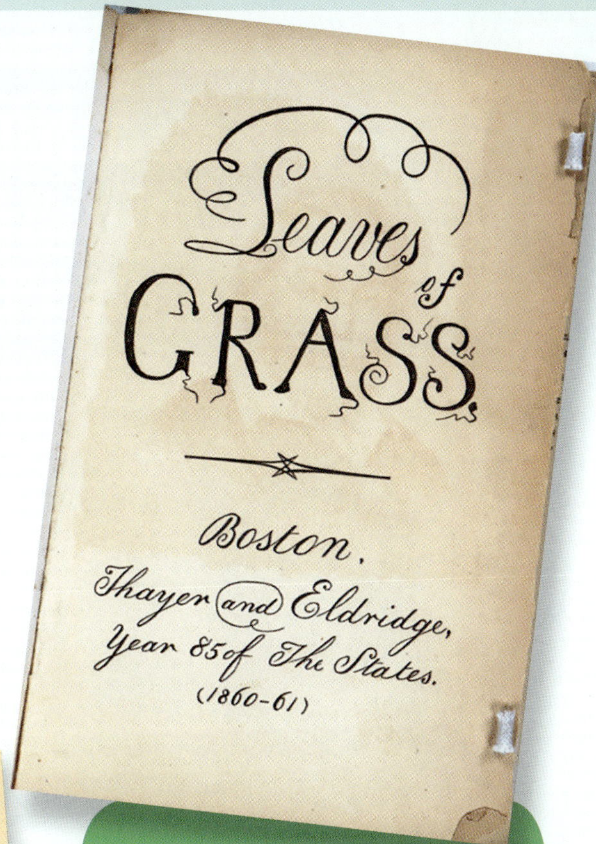

12

Poems in the first edition of *Leaves of Grass*

- The second edition had 32 poems.
- *Drum-Taps* is a collection of Whitman's poems about the Civil War.
- The ninth and final edition of *Leaves of Grass* was published in 1892. It included nearly 400 poems.

7 Elizabeth Barrett Browning: Poet of Love and Causes

Elizabeth Barrett Browning.

English poet Elizabeth Barrett Browning was born in 1806. From an early age, she read and wrote poems. Before she was even a teen, she wrote "The Battle of Marathon." This epic poem told of a battle between the ancient Greeks and Persians.

Browning's early poems were often about classical literature. But she eventually wrote about human rights issues. She wrote poems on the wrongs of slavery. She also wrote about children being forced to work in mines and factories. Browning's work often addressed the social issues of her day. Sometimes this made her unpopular. But critics admired her talents as a poet.

Her book *Poems* was published in 1844. It gained the attention of fellow poet Robert Browning. They would marry a couple of years later. Then, in 1850, Browning published *Sonnets from the Portuguese.* Many of its poems were dedicated to her husband. This collection included "How Do I Love Thee?

SONNETS

The sonnet is a poetry form developed in Italy in the 1200s. Poets like William Shakespeare made sonnets popular in England in the 1500s. Sonnets have 14 lines and are very lyrical. They have a rhythmic meter and rhyme scheme. Love is often their subject.

I See thine image through my tears to
night, Ayd yet to-day I saw thee
smiling
How Rfer the
cause?
Belove
d, is it
thou O
r I, who
makes
me
sad
The seafyte Amid the chanted joy and
thankful rite May so fall flat, with pale
insensate brow, On the altar-stair.
I hear thy voice and vow, Perplexed, uu
certain, since thou art out of sight,
As he, in his swooning ears, the choir's
amen. Beloved, dost thou love?
or did I see all The glory as I
dreamed, and fainted when
Too vehement light dilated
my ideal, For my soul's eyes?
Will that light come again, As
now these tears come—falling hot and
real?
Sonnet 30

(Sonnet 43)." It is probably her best-known poem. It starts like this:

How do I love thee? Let me count the ways.
I love thee to the depth and breadth and height
My soul can reach ...

Browning died in 1861. Today, she is best known for her many love poems.

573

Number of love letters Elizabeth and Robert Browning shared before marrying

- Robert Browning wrote the poem "The Pied Piper of Hamelin."
- The Brownings' letters were turned into a play. It was titled *The Barretts of Wimpole Street.*
- Browning was a sickly child. She was often bedridden.

Elizabeth and her husband, Robert, in 1853.

8

Emily Dickinson: A Shy Poet with a Unique Voice

Emily Dickinson between 1846 and 1847.

Two poets helped define American poetry. They were Walt Whitman and Emily Dickinson. Both lived about the same time. Both have very unique voices.

Dickinson was born in 1830 in Amherst, Massachusetts. She grew up reading the works of English poets, from John Keats to Elizabeth Barrett Browning. At the time, there were few American poets. Dickinson was a recluse. She spent much of her time at home. She rarely traveled or visited friends. Because of this, many of her poems were about longing and loneliness.

Dickinson wrote many letters to family members and friends. She often included poems. One of her friends was the editor Samuel Bowles. He published several of her poems in the *Springfield Republican* newspaper. But all were published without her name. Other friends were writers who encouraged her to write.

Dickinson's poems were usually short. But they were packed with meaning. They provided personal observations of nature and society. Much of her writing was also intensely emotional. Her poetic voice was unique for the time. Many of her

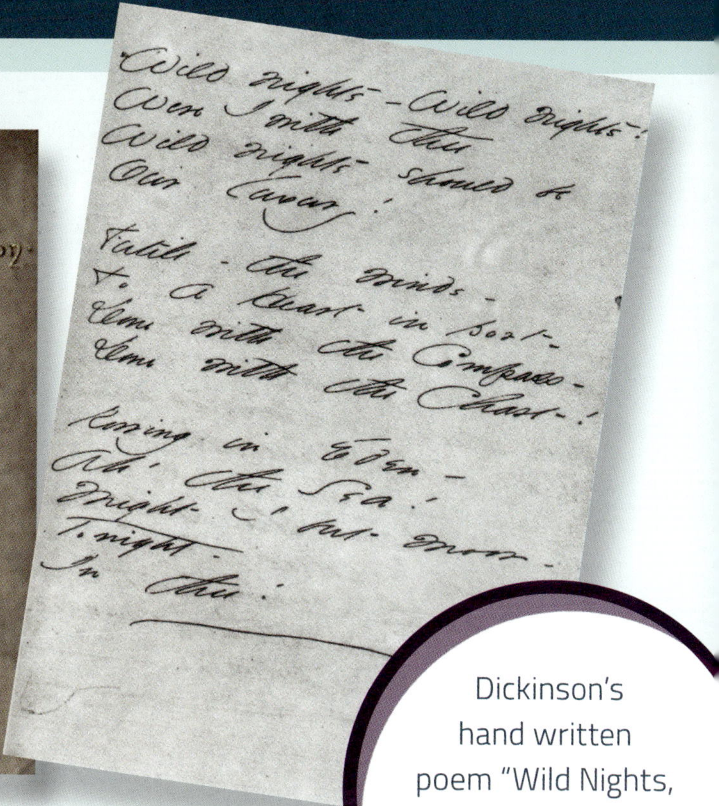

Dickinson's hand written poem "Wild Nights, Wild Nights" where dash marks are visible.

poems contain strange dash marks. No one is quite sure what they are for.

Dickinson died in 1886. The first book of her poetry was published four years later. She has since become recognized as one of America's greatest poets.

THINK ABOUT IT

Emily Dickinson did not learn to write poetry at school. Instead, she read poetry books. She also talked to other poets. How would this help her learn to write poetry?

40

Number of homemade books in which Emily Dickinson copied her poems

- She made them herself from folded sheets of paper and thread.
- They contain about 800 poems.
- Only about 10 of Dickinson's poems were published during her lifetime.

9

Pablo Neruda: The People's Poet

Pablo Neruda in 1963.

14

Number of lines in a sonnet

- Neruda published his first book of poetry, *Crepusculario*, in 1923. The word *crepusculario* means "twilight."
- He spent several years in exile because of his political views.
- In 1971, Neruda won the Nobel Prize for Literature.

Ricardo Eliecer Neftalí Reyes Basoalto was born in 1904 in Chile. His family did not support his writing. So when he published his first poems, he used a pen name. He called himself Pablo Neruda.

Neruda established himself as a poet early in life. His love sonnets were especially popular. They were seen as very loving and passionate poems. Several are included in *Twenty Love Poems and a Song of Despair*. Published in 1924, this collection made Neruda a star. It is still his best-known work. It also is the best-selling poetry book in Spanish. It has been translated into many languages and has sold more than 20 million copies.

Neruda was more than just a poet. He was also a politician. For several years, he worked at various positions in the Chilean government. This allowed him to travel. During his travels, he witnessed the struggles of workers around the world. His poems began to reflect the social issues he saw. He was seen as a poet of the people because he supported workers. The World Peace Council awarded Neruda the International Peace Prize in 1950.

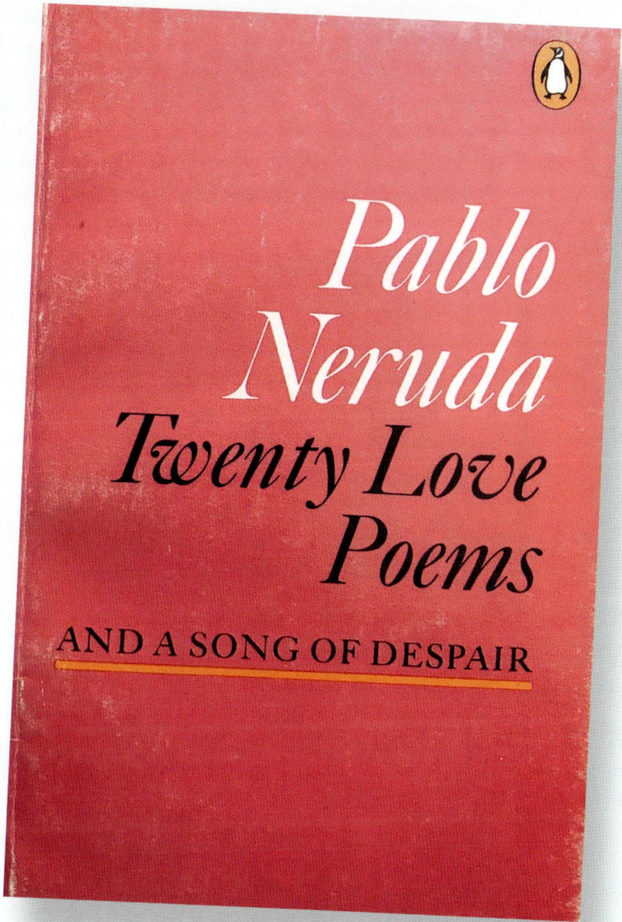

Neruda died in 1973. He is considered one of the greatest Latin poets.

THINK ABOUT IT

Poets like Neruda comment on politics in their poetry. Do you think poets should write about politics and other social issues? Why or why not?

10

Sylvia Plath: Confessional Poet

Sylvia Plath in 1961.

Sylvia Plath was born in 1932 in Boston, Massachusetts. She was only eight years old when her father died. Her struggles with his passing would greatly affect her poetry. Perhaps her best-known poem is "Daddy." The poem starts with a lot of words that sound similar. Plath uses "you," "do," "shoe," and "achoo." Together, they sound angry and give the poem a personal feeling. That trait would be common in much of her work.

Plath's poems were filled with raw emotion. She wrote about her mental illness, self-doubt, and unhappy marriage. Her poems gave people glimpses into her life and thoughts. This type of poetry is called confessional poetry.

The poem "Daddy" was published in Plath's first book, *The Colossus and Other Poems*. It came out in 1960. This was the only book of her poems published while she was alive. In 1963, she took her own life. By then, she was one of the most critically acclaimed poets in the United States.

Plath's only novel, *The Bell Jar*, was originally published in 1963 under her pseudonym "Victoria Lucas."

CONFESSIONAL POETRY

Confessional poetry became popular in the late 1950s. It touched on personal subjects that poets usually did not write about. Confessional poets wrote about their private lives and personal experiences. Along with Plath, Anne Sexton and Robert Lowell are two well-known confessional poets.

8

Sylvia Plath's age when her first poem was published

- "Poem" was published in the children's section of the *Boston Herald*.
- Plath also wrote a novel called *The Bell Jar*. It tells the story of a woman who wants to be a poet.
- *Ariel* was Plath's second book of poetry. It came out two years after her death.

11

Gwendolyn Brooks: Poet of Black Culture

Gwendolyn Brooks in 1945.

Gwendolyn Brooks was born in 1917 in Topeka, Kansas. Shortly afterward, her family moved to Chicago. Brooks grew up loving to read and write. As a teenager, she published poems in a popular African American newspaper, *Chicago Defender*. Her first book, *A Street in Bronzeville*, came out in 1945. Her poems portrayed the lives of African Americans.

Brooks lived during a time of segregation. African Americans were not allowed to eat in the same restaurants as whites. They could not use the same restrooms. Her own experiences with racism helped shape her writing. She often wrote about the struggles of African Americans. Her poems told how many of them lived in poverty.

In 1945, Brooks published her second book, *Annie Allen*. This collection told the story of an African American girl growing up in Chicago. Critics thought it was an incredibly original book. It also earned her the Pulitzer Prize in poetry. She was the first African American to win this major literary award.

Brooks died in 2003. Throughout her life, she shone a light on the lives of everyday African Americans.

Brooks visits with young poetry award winners at the University of Chicago in 1981.

POET LAUREATE

The poet laureate of the United States is the nation's official poet. Their full title is Poet Laureate Consultant in Poetry to the Library of Congress. Their job is to grow the American people's interest in reading and writing poetry. Louise Bogan was the first woman poet laureate. Robert Hayden was the first African American. Juan Felipe Herrera was the first Latino.

13

Gwendolyn Brooks's age when her first poem was published

- "Eventide" appeared in *American Childhood* magazine.
- Brooks wrote more than 20 books.
- In 1985, she became the first African American poet laureate of the United States.

12

Dennis Brutus: Activist Poet

Dennis Brutus was more than a poet. He was also a teacher and an activist. Brutus was born in 1924 in what is now Zimbabwe. When he was five, his family moved to South Africa, where his parents were from.

At the time, a white minority ruled the country. Strict apartheid policies were the law. People were segregated based on their race. Whites and blacks could not go to school together. They could not play on the same sports teams. There were places blacks were not allowed to go, and things they could not to do.

Dennis Brutus in 1967.

Brutus protested these practices. He started a committee to allow black South African athletes to compete in the Olympic games. The government tried to silence Brutus. They fired him from his job as a high school teacher. They told him not to write or speak against apartheid.

But Brutus did not stop. He wrote poems like "A Poem about Sharpeville." It tells of a massacre in the small town of Sharpeville in 1960. Police killed 69 black protesters. Many others were injured. These included children.

1963

Year when Dennis Brutus published his first book of poems, *Sirens, Knuckles, and Boots*

- Brutus was in jail when his first book appeared.
- Brutus's prison cell was next to Nelson Mandela's. Mandela had also protested apartheid. He would eventually become president of South Africa.
- Brutus wrote about his time in jail in a collection of poems called *Simple Lust*.

For continuing to voice his opinions, Brutus was imprisoned. He spent 18 months in jail. Afterward, he fled South Africa. He eventually moved to the United States. There, he continued to write about the injustices of segregation.

Brutus died in 2009. His voice of protest helped end apartheid in South Africa.

Brutus at a protest in 2000.

More Poets to Know

Virgil

Virgil was a poet of ancient Rome. He was born in 70 BCE. His most famous work is the *Aeneid*. This epic poem tells the myth of how the Roman empire was founded. It starts with the adventures of Aeneas. He was a Trojan prince who escaped Troy after the Greeks conquered the city. On his way to Italy, Aeneas faced monsters and fought many battles. The book ends with Aeneas defeating the Latins, the people of Italy.

Chaucer

Geoffrey Chaucer was an English poet born in the 1340s. He lived during a time when literature was usually not written in English. But the popularity of Chaucer's work helped change that. His best-known book is *The Canterbury Tales*. It is a collection of stories about a group of pilgrims on their way to the Canterbury Cathedral.

Geoffrey Chaucer.

Mary Oliver

Mary Oliver was an American poet born in 1935. Much of her poetry is about nature. She also famously said that poetry shouldn't be fancy. She believed it should be written so everyday people can understand it. Oliver won a Pulitzer Prize for her book of poetry *American Primitive*. She received a National Book Award for *White Pines*.

Tracy K. Smith in 2017.

Tracy K. Smith

Tracy K. Smith is an American poet born in 1972. Her poetry often focuses on pop culture. The poems in *Life on Mars* include many references to popular science fiction movies. This book also won a Pulitzer Prize. In 2017, Smith was named the poet laureate of the United States.

Glossary

apartheid
A social system where black people do not have the same rights as white people.

enlightenment
The highest possible spiritual state.

epic poem
A long poem that tells a story.

literature
Written works, such as poems and novels.

lyric or lyrical poem
A songlike poem that expresses personal feelings.

meter
The pattern, or rhythm, of beats in a poem.

myth
A traditional story.

oral
By word of mouth.

preface
The introduction to a book.

Renaissance
The period of European history that followed the Middle Ages. The Renaissance is known as a time of great development in the arts and sciences.

segregated
Separated by race or gender.

tradition
A set of beliefs and customs that are handed down from one generation to the next.

Read More

Agrimbau, Diego, and Marcelo Zamora. *Homer's The Iliad: A Graphic Novel.* North Mankato, MN: Stone Arch Books, 2018.

Berne, Jennifer. *On Wings of Words: The Extraordinary Life of Emily Dickinson.* San Francisco, CA: Chronicle Books, 2019.

Bodden, Valerie. *Finding the Rhyme in a Poem.* Mankato, MN: Creative Education, 2016.

Loewen, Nancy. *Walt Whitman.* Mankato, MN: Creative Education, 2014.

Slade, Suzanne. *Exquisite: The Poetry and Life of Gwendolyn Brooks.* New York: Abrams Books for Young Readers, 2019.

Index

About the Author

Allan Morey grew up in central Wisconsin but now lives in St. Paul, Minnesota, with his wife and two dogs, Stitch and Ty. He has written many books for children, and especially enjoys writing about technology, sports, and art.